D0071662

ACCLAIM FOR DEREK HINES'S

# Gilgamesh

"Hines's energetic metaphors and nimble wit revivify the thrill of a very old tale." —*The Times* (London)

"An evocative lyric journey through the Mesopotamian story, glittering with Hines's own fresh images."
—*Financial Times*

"A sparkling poetic vision." —*The Oxford Times*

"Impressive, consistent . . . packed with good things."
—Christopher Logue

"I read this version with great interest and admiration. It has real energy and drive with some splendidly interesting images. I was held throughout."
—Ian Hamilton

"A superb achievement. The cinematic swoops, that terrific, loss-haunted elegy, absolutely packed with reverberating phrases. . . . It is not only a rendering of the poem but a brilliant, vital contemporary commentary on it." —Paul Newman, editor, *Abraxis*

DERREK HINES

# Gilgamesh

Derrek Hines was born and raised in Canada and read
Ancient Near Eastern Studies at university. He has
won prizes in, among others, the National Poetry
Competition and the Arvon Foundation International
Competition, and has published two books of poetry.
He lives on the Lizard Peninsula in Cornwall, England.

ALSO BY DERREK HINES

*Van Norden*

*Open to the Weather* (with Alice Kavounas)

# Gilgamesh

DERREK HINES

*Anchor Books*

A DIVISION OF RANDOM HOUSE, INC.

NEW YORK

FIRST ANCHOR BOOKS EDITION, OCTOBER 2004

Copyright © 2002 by Derrek Hines

All rights reserved under International and Pan-American
Copyright Conventions. Published in the United States by
Anchor Books, a division of Random House, Inc., New York,
and in Canada by Random House of Canada Limited,
Toronto. Originally published in Great Britain
by Chatto & Windus, London, in 2002.

Anchor Books and colophon are registered trademarks
of Random House, Inc.

Library of Congress Cataloging-in-Publication Data
Hines, Derrek.
Gilgamesh / Derrek Hines.
p. cm.
ISBN: 1-4000-7733-8
1. Gilgamesh–Adaptations.
2. Epic poetry, Assyro-Babylonian–Adaptations.
3. Erech (Extinct city)–Kings and rulers–Poetry.
I. Gilgamesh. II. Title.
PR9199.4.H56G55   2004
811'.6–dc22   20040464415

www.anchorbooks.com

Printed in the United States of America
10  9  8  7  6  5  4  3  2  1

*This book is dedicated to*
*June*

CENTRAL ARKANSAS LIBRARY SYSTEM
LITTLE ROCK PUBLIC LIBRARY
100 ROCK STREET
LITTLE ROCK, ARKANSAS 72201

# ACKNOWLEDGMENTS

I wish to thank all those friends who supported me in this work; and also my editor, Rebecca Carter, for her encouragement. The suggestions for improvements from Alice Kavounas and Diane Johnstone are above thanks. None of this would have been possible without the untiring support of my wife, Joanna Hines.

CENTRAL ARKANSAS LIBRARY SYSTEM
LITTLE ROCK PUBLIC LIBRARY
100 ROCK STREET
LITTLE ROCK, ARKANSAS 72201

# CONTENTS

# INTRODUCTION

The *Epic of Gilgamesh* is the first great book of man's heart. The original epic derived from an oral version and was written in Sumerian, the language of the people who lived in what is now southern Mesopotamia, in cuneiform on clay tablets about 2100 BC. Eventually, as Semitic-speaking peoples moved down from the north, the poem was translated into their language, Akkadian, which became the lingua franca of the ancient world for almost two thousand years. The *Epic of Gilgamesh* became a standard text, copied by scribes throughout the Near East, rather as Homer and Ovid would be centuries later.

The poem enthralled the ancient world as it does ours because it touches on the themes of our common humanity: love, death and friendship. It is the story of a mortal defying fate, and of the harrowing of Hell by a hero in his search for immortality. And finally, there is a suggestion of something transcendent, beyond death, in a brief elevation of man above the gods.

Each generation discovers and reinterprets the mysteries of past literature. Shakespeare reworked the Latin historians, Pope in the eighteenth century translated Homer; in our time Ted Hughes has written a version of *Ovid*, Christopher Logue the

*Iliad*, and Seamus Heaney *Beowulf*. My poem is an interpretation of the *Epic of Gilgamesh*, but is in no sense a translation. While not changing the essentials of the narrative, I have added material in an effort to recapture for the modern reader some of the vigour and excitement the original audience must have felt.

In this poem mankind first glimpsed its fate in the mirror of literature, and that image became a blueprint that influenced Homer and, through him, the later classical poets and the writers of the west.

### An Outline of the Received Text

Two-thirds divine, Gilgamesh, King of Uruk, oppresses his people. They especially resent his claim to the first night with any bride before the husband. The gods hear his subjects' plea for justice and create Enkidu, a wild man set to roam the wastelands until summoned to tame the King. Shamhat, a hierodule or sacred prostitute of the goddess of love Ishtar, is sent out into the desert to instruct Enkidu in sex and civilisation. She does. He likes it. They travel to Uruk, Enkidu intent on putting an end to Gilgamesh's abuses. The two heroes meet in the dark streets and wrestle. Although evenly matched, Enkidu defers to his opponent's sovereignty and they become friends.

Great deeds follow. The friends, in violation of divine laws, journey to Lebanon to cut the sacred cedar for Uruk's temple doors; in the process they kill Humbaba, a sort of wizard protecting the trees. On their return, Ishtar falls in love with Gilgamesh; but he, knowing her other husbands have ended up either dead or transformed into beasts, refuses her. In her wrath she appeals to Anu, High Lord of Heaven, for revenge, and wins from him the right to bring down the Bull of Heaven (the constellation Taurus) to destroy Gilgamesh. Nothing daunted, our heroes dispatch it at the price of committing sacrilege.

The gods in plenum session decide this junketing must stop and debate which man should die. Some suggest Gilgamesh; but the council chooses Enkidu, who, after a dream in which he foresees his end, dies.

Gilgamesh is broken, and there follows the first great lament for a dead companion in literature.

Inconsolable, and desperate to find the immortality he feels his semi-divine status should confer, Gilgamesh wanders for years. Finally he arrives at a tavern by the sea run by Shiduri, a wise goddess, who suggests he approach the boatman Ur-shanabi, who can cross the waters of Death. Gilgamesh persuades him to ferry him to the Underworld where he speaks with Uta-napishti, the Sumerian Noah, who survived the Flood and was given immortality. Although Gilgamesh's own plea is refused by the gods, Uta-napishti gifts him the Herb of Rejuvenation, which, on Gilgamesh's return to the upper world, is stolen by a serpent. Resigned to his destiny, Gilgamesh returns to Uruk and prepares for death.

I have used many sources and translations of the epic. The most comprehensive, containing both the standard Akkadian version and the Sumerian texts, is the excellent scholarly translation by Andrew George, *The Epic of Gilgamesh: A New Translation* (London: Allen Lane, 1999).

DBH

# Beginnings

Here is Gilgàmesh, king of Uruk:
two-thirds divine, a mummy's boy,
zeppelin ego, cock like a trip-hammer,
and solid chrome, no-prisoners arrogance.

Pulls women like beer rings.
Grunts when puzzled.
A bully. A jock. Perfecto. But in love? –
a moon-calf, and worse, thoughtful.

Next, a one-off:
clay and lightning entangled by the gods
to create a strong-man from the wastelands
to curb Gilgamesh – named Enkìdu.

Sour electric fear, desert mirage at your throat,
strong enough to hold back the night,
so handsome he robs the world of horizon –
for no one's gaze lifts beyond him.

Gilgamesh and Enkidu stand
astride the threshold of history at Sumer.

Five thousand years,
Ishtar's skirts,
five thousand years are gathered aside
so we enter the view from Uruk's palace:

Euphrates' airy, fish-woven halls,
a sleep of reed beds, the éclat of date palms,
wind-glossed corn. And in the distance

desert – the sun's loose gunpowder.
Green rolls up
and rasps along it like a tongue
wetting sandpaper.

Here and there,
jostling with the fast-forward business
on the quays, spiralling above the potter's wheel,
buoyed by the clatter of café gossip:

up-drafts of ideas, thermals of invention.

For the cut of every thought here
is new for our race, and tart with novelty.

Then look: footprints of the mind's bird
in its take-off scramble across wet clay tablets.
Writing!

It was also time
when, just as the lemon tree's greenroom
sweats with auditions for tomorrow's sun,
the world swelled with potential heroes.

Have there been two such
as Gilgamesh and Enkidu
who released our first imagination
to map the new interior spaces we still
scribble on the backs of envelopes, of lives?

They strode into deeds like furnaces
to flash off the husk of their humanity,
and emerged, purified of time.


Now like a burning-glass Enkidu's wildness
is focusing the people's discontent
into dust devils of rumour
that scour through the city.

The Trapper is sent out,
ordered to hire a temple prostitute,
'a garment of Ishtar'; lead her into the desert
to civilise Enkidu – net him
to quell Gilgamesh.

3

# Shamhat of the April Gate

What do we know of sacred harlots?
What's sacred that sweeps through our lives?
Enter Shamhat, who can be bought like a beer
from the stall outside the temple gate.

Take her then as the whole, hired
month of April, of the gods' Now;
not as equivalence but the month,
harlot as might be April;

Shamhat as might be a modern woman
slouched over a back-street bistro table
her breasts too small to shadow yet,
and in her bruises almost overdressed;
skinny enough to dilute
the whisky-neon dawn.

A cup of sleet, a grubby
two-cigarette mantra
against the ache of breaching
in her sex:

4

the month's raw, self-greasing tubers
forcing up into shoots
the sap's hot green ether.

And the drag-chute of Spring's afterbirth
nicked on the wind's thorn.
Cruel, cruellest and . . .

a rag of love-things in free fall
in her heart that shouldn't be here,
like a man

– like this one, the Trapper,
who draws her as the moon the slake-tide,
through the desert
to water Enkidu's lime-dry throat.

All the men who crutched her belly on bedsteads,
gorged her, ground her hips above the grave's
mattress, stand with her now.

'I am Shamhat.' She fingers Enkidu's tangled hair.
(A pro: her flashgun smile will develop
to red-eye, his lust-eye.)


You have seen a cottage by the sea,
white, lap-built against the spray,
paused in the lilt of dunes
like a skiff with feathered oars,
its darkness waiting for summer.

Then the shucking of winter shutters;
the abrupt gush and gulp of light
quenching a thirsting interior
like un-boarding an old fountain:
thus Enkidu's soul at Shamhat's touch.

And his sadness, suddenly aware of what he is,
a fumble of doubts and longings.

'I am Shamhat.
Part my gown and the keys at my girdle
that undo whore, undo mother, saint,
to reveal the eternal carcass tipped in the beauty
of the dunghill or the star-breeding towers in Orion.'

To Enkidu, who has known
no other woman, she is beautiful.

From the ruined face
the gentle voice, like a buddleia
flowering through a derelict factory's window.

His fingers, calloused by freedom,
struggle like netted birds
with the breathy sea-cotton of her layers
(O my first woman!):

the wonder and nuzzle of breasts,
the notch that baits men
as iron filings are drawn to fur a magnet.

Finally Shamhat gasped a full-throated
praise of male hydraulics,
entering her like the stiff *shaduf*
that lifts night's constellations off the river's face,
spilling wet star-seed into the splayed canals.

After seven nights of love,
as a man might,
Enkidu lost his understanding of animal speech.
But it was a fair trade.

# The Meeting

D<sub>ay</sub>
    descends;
              a hem (a garter?) now her thigh
                                     eases
into the nevermore of dusk's entropy;

and she looks back over her shoulder,
up through the lush flip-book
of her farewells.

A line of crushed light remains above the horizon
as if the shutters on a jeweller's window
had jammed an inch shy of closing;

space enough
to allow Enkidu and Shamhat
to materialise before Uruk's gate.

Street urchins gawk; donkeys absorb.
A town guide peels from the shadows,
approaches, and falls back in awe.

Enkidu has come to strip Gilgamesh
of his right to taste the bride before the husband.
The foundry of his anger quakes and glows.


They push through the streets without torches;
Shamhat, three paces behind,
lights his way.

Enkidu is troubled, his anger flawed.
Doubt tears at certainty –
a risk the self-righteous must take –
for what he expects
he might not find.

But her? Watch her. She is changing,
uncloaking from a chrysalis of desert calico
that shimmers and wings to silk in her slipstream
a hundred feet into air
borrowed from Heaven.

The volume of her presence
soars beyond the audible;
she reveals herself like a female Odysseus
transfixing the suitors;

bursts from Penelope's weaving,
and with her swarm
the hungry threads of power.

She is no longer the 'garment of Ishtar'
but its very owner, striding down
the cat-walk of Uruk's high street
in the designer gowns of Paradise,
Ishtar's high priestess, Goddess incarnate;
so briefly glimpsed in passing,
the grace of her,
like snow touching warm ground.

Hip to hip, Shamhat and light,
part the darkness; of the two
she is the more radiant.

Enkidu sees none of this;
broods and stomps on.

Soft-mouthed as a gundog
dark retrieves these few sounds:
a clatter of supper plates,
the dry thresh, like a woman's stockings,
of palm fronds,

the rustle of moonlight, rinsing itself
up to its wrists in the river.


Across town, Gilgamesh
sets off to split a bride's veil
while the groom groans white with shame.
His right? Divine right, power right.
In reverse order.

Around him in the swelter-light
smuts off reed torches cling
to the sweating skin of his young bucks,
the town's *jeunesse dorée*,
nervy as water splattered on hot oil;
too drunk for honour, but hoping
for woman-scraps from his table.

He has corrupted their worth
with his vanity, yet
they mime his airs, ape his swagger,
try on his used breath

to live second-hand,
hand-me-down time,
always in fear of that whetted anger,
half-drawn in his pride's sheath.

To him they are means.
Gilgamesh squats on Uruk's soul.


A messenger stands before the king,
his mouth working like a boated trout,
or a seer fresh out of prophecy.
Silence, a bolt, rigid in the throat.
Empty cups of faces turn to Gilgamesh.

Instantly everything is known –
the news clamps jump-cables to them
and throws a switch – a current arcs and spits

between Gilgamesh here,
and Enkidu at the April Gate,
galvanising the town.


Talk dries in the cafés,
as when the soldiers of an occupation
enter a restaurant, and a coded silence
becomes speech. Where silence is language,
meaning is everywhere.

The people let fear think for them;
fear steals their thought and makes bold.
They watch Gilgamesh pass,
and chant under their breath,

like football fans from the terraces:
*Dead. End. Cul-de-sac.*
*Dead. End. Cul-de-sac.*


Still, as the heroes stumble into their roles,
there is someone, as always, disconnected –
someone whistling as he repairs a pot –

unmindful of the great events at his elbow
like the ploughman oblivious in Brueghel's
*Fall of Icarus.*

It is done; they accelerate towards each other
welded to Destiny's tram rails: two black cores
hungry for the other's light.

Juggernauts too wide for the narrow streets
they spew tall coxcombs of sparks
as they grind against the buildings.
They meet in the square, and stop.

Haste scissors off their clothes:

Enkidu's furs, drop and crouch;

the king's double silks (light blue, indigo,
like the two breezes off opposed seas
which ruffle the sheep's fleece on Hellespont)

faint to the ground –

both men now qualities of moonlight.

Sudden jostling in the crowd:
the fight is hijacked by the expectations
of spectacle – *paparazzi*:
flashbulbs sun the moon aside
carving a tableau, a stark iconography
of function without emotion.

The contestants are burnished gold-leaf,
wetted crimson in the glare;
heraldic beasts on a carousel,
huge, stupid with encoded exhibition.

They topple into each other
like the Empire State and Chrysler buildings;
their hearts trapped in the elevators,
their minds locked in the blueprints
of testosterone flush and muscle.

Fierce, so saturated, dense with power, they are become
a gravity: voices and light bend nearing them.
They drain cities of energy from each other
and draw on more: distant Lakish dims,
Ur browns out . . .


Until, from behind the crowd, Shamhat speaks.
Only the wrestlers hear her voice,
200 cubic miles of summer storm, compressed,
compressed: − it begins as

a wet finger rubbed around the rim of a wine glass;
increases to a whisper, gears up to a rumble
circling a bronze chamber in their heads −
faster − until the words burst in their skulls:

THE GODS ORDAIN FRIENDSHIP.

Anger is reversed so violently
they are motion sick with the change

and the challenge of foreignness,
as when, in the uncertainty of abroad,
you find you are a question,
not the answer you thought yourself to be.

Backwards from the clinch, dream-escaping;
smile into eyes . . .

The crowd murmurs, restive with discontent.
A formula has been betrayed. The fight ends
not in justice as they expected:
Shamhat imposed the epiphany of recognition,
which is greater than justice and love.
But it is not resolution.


Gilgamesh takes one heady step, two;
living for the first time
for someone else.

# Gilgamesh's Hymn to Morning

See, dawn breathes into . . . the flaws:

rumour behind bitumen,
false-dawn cock crow, current surge . . .
Dark's unstable touch-paper splutters
and launches the invention of

SUN – gold vaporised at dew point
flash-plating the river's laid steel.


'O, great spinnaker of morning,
bellied by a wind
taller than the meadows of Orion,

that pulls into its cavitation thought –
the spindrift off the impossible –
the first draw of worked, imaginable space

that roils and oils and charms mind
into a downright love of it.

For is thought not the greatest mystery,
and imagination a metaphor
for its beauty and wonder?


'Come, my brother –
a broad jest of sunlight
clowns on the sills of day

just as we entertain the gods,
our doings like oar-prints
filling with the provinces of Heaven.

And all is written: Fate already chalked
on the lofting floor, the theorems of grace,
the tracings of wind's plumed assumption.
Lift your arms and sail.


'Listen: noon
evaporates from the water-clock;
noon, on the slack–clutched river

where light lists a degree, furls and crumples
like a xebec shrugging its sails off the wind.

This is honey time, Enkidu,
and we stand braced on the walls of Uruk
as at the kerb of dreams.
Let us tread them like gods,

for, my friend, such days are gifts,
victories over the immense indifference.

We will inhale this, our life's dawn
evaporating off a god's brow; grasp time by its scruff;
brave the entry-only land of the hero,

and not return: for once we've stepped into it,
the people never allow the hero
to be a part of them again.

There we are to capture for thought,
unmarked, stateless spaces in the mind,
and leave them outside the walls for mankind.'


Heroes. Consider, reader: heroes.
The whole idea waiting to abuse itself.
The modernist in us undercutting
everything to be said here,
with that taste for the corruption of the ideal,
the soured, smug edge of bankrupt irony
defending us from belief, that 'safety in derision'.

We can be ironical with the matter of the issue,
but not its spirit.      That
inhales dawns.

# The Humbaba Campaign

## (A soldier's diary)

The councillors were dead against the madness –
a thousand miles to Lebanon for cedar
and squander the toff's precious Hooray Henrys
against Humbaba's troops . . .

But our lord Gilgamesh strutted and harangued:
shrivel-calves, rattle-scrotums,
fear's banquet, etc.

A dark voice, tar brushed over rust.
We clocked there was something rotten.

The while he was glancing at pretty-boy Enkidu.
You could see that edged glint in their eyes.
They got off on it,
egging each other on, dicks on the table.

Cedar for the temple doors, my ass.
It's glory's hard-on for those two,
and no mind for us. Bastards.

We were at ease in ranks for all this,
with no idea who Humbaba was; but the corporal
turned pale as blanco: 'He's the worst,
worse than watching your children burn alive
and surviving it. If we live after this show

we'll carry a hell even death won't ease.
He's a wizard, a quantum entanglement magus,
set by Enlil, Fate Maker,
to guard the Sacred Cedars in Lebanon.'

So, we figured, no snatch for medals in this caper.


A month now, desert-yomping in full kit.
Scorpion wind in the face, crotch rot, boils.
Not helped by our great King, who wakes each morning
from dreams like multiple car crashes –
a bloody Cassandra weeping catastrophe,
until Enkidu talks him round.


In the valley of the Bekaa under Mt Lebanon.
Easy soldiering with the ladies willing,
their legs spread wide as a peal of bells;

plenty of grub, and the zig of split-stone fences
snaking through terraced orchards,
apple and Eve ready.
Good, rolling chariot country.

The foothills. Our yeomanry
got stuck into Humbaba's lot this morning.
We watched them shake out
into order of battle, advancing at a stroll
up the meadow towards the forest

as they dressed to the right,
like a list of names justifying into columns
for the face of a war memorial.

Three hundred yards beyond return
the telegram-maker of enemy fire
scythed out from the tree-line,
and the ranks started to crumple.

Men dying into grass;
all those souls whistling past our heads,
homewards.


We supported the chariots today –
soft-shelled tanks on a leash,
desperate to harden with speed,
but forced to slow into single file through the woods,
soft again.

Everyone screwed up to pitch; the recruits
like twists of green gunpowder.
From the flank we watched the ambush's fusillade
sieve most of them to Hell

and the chariot column, broken-backed
like a garbled sentence,
punctuated as the rounds smacked home:

men stiffened to exclamation, curled to question,
toppled to period.

We targeted an enemy marksman, but it wasn't human,
the first of Humbaba's Auras we'd seen –
sometimes light shone through him
in the cedar dapple, sometimes not – his aim

blocked for a moment like a telephone
waiting to be connected . . . was . . .

our Captain of Chariots shuddered on to tiptoes,
and died, dazzled by an attack from the sun,
a life's length from earth, like a fighter pilot.

We fell back, dug in.
Next dawn he was still there;
you felt the search-pressure of his sniper's mind
like a breeze as it quartered the front,

weighed the calculations:
a pound of distance, an ounce of windage.
Silence on half-cock.

But in the horizontal light
he reached to clear a lisp of gossamer
from his rifle muzzle, and the corp nailed him.

What are these Auras?
It breaks our teeth to think of them.
Psychic assassins? Zombies?
Tough as the Schutzstaffel though.

They come at us from everywhere: we are killed
out of friends' faces,

or dragged out from under our actor's paint
(those that were extras in the Shamhat episode).
Barbed wire branded on the backs of our eyelids
so there's no escape in sleep – no sleep in a trench

with a friend's snoring lung wound.


We are enspelled here, deep in the forest-sea swell
where men rise to aim in the strangeness,
and drown.
Hand to hand for every tree,
concussed for days as the mortar's blunt snout

roots and turns us inside out;
by day shattering the Sun, Venus by night.


New boy stopped a grenade today.
We sluiced what remained from his armour
as you'd pressure-hose mud from a wheel arch.

The platoon's half-splintered
like a flailed hedge;
handcuffed to a Niagara of fear.

Orders, counter orders;
undergrowth like hooked drift-nets;
and these goddam trees like rain-blistered
gas capes, drip and wheeze and whisper fog.

What're we doing here anyway?
This is God-land, verboten;
piss-yourself-with-terror land.


The lieutenant bought it twice.
We'd left him two hundred yards to the rear
for morning burial, but a plasma bolt

overshot and fried him, fisting a million volts
down his spine. He arched and crackled
like a rainbow;

brain kick-started
like a panicked Lazarus –
so he jumped up, hobbled in grave-clothes,
and lurched, x-legged a few steps,

out of the ranks of the dead.
Gently sir, gently; remember
the one-off drill, fall in again
with the ghost-boys.        Lucky bugger.

Why didn't they tell us about this wire,
the enfilading strong point the onagers missed?
Why do they never?

We're charging Humbaba's bunker.
I make it over the wire with a boot-hold
in the sarge's oath-clagged mouth –
not that he was going to need it,
hanging there all gut-shot and scrag-end of neck.
Air shattering like plate glass
against your face. Brisk, brisk.


Here is how others saw the fight –
the world's first in armour: binding joints,
shouts for oil cans, and the pan-
demonium of men vortexed in battle;
a ten-storey concrete stairwell
down which banshees: sheet-metal, cutlery, hands.
Dub in grunts, pleas, blood-coughs;
worse, the butterfly impact of dying gasps:
try to stand upright in their shock.

See one stagger from the hammering,
his heart-knot snipped, totter, as though
he was juggling life like ten thousand gallons
of loose water on his shoulders.

And others, encore, encore, and, oh,
they spill it all.

Now learn how silence rippled over the battle;
how it approached like a wind across the sea
seen from a cliff: far out a down-draught

spawls and shivers the surface, another,
closer, another, like footprints, until
the first breeze leans on the face. Then she distilled

to the most beautiful human you have seen –
or, pillow-hugging, dreamed – and came on slowly,
undressing sound from air.
The loss of each garment sleeps, sword, anger.
Warriors are dumbfound, time-blank,
birds nest in their mouths; by ranks, swathes,
the field falls silent, still glossed with surprise
like fresh-mown hay.

Except for the shape-shifting Humbaba
who squats in a nest of corpses,
one pincer of his crab-like arms
drumming his shield; and higher, gelding screams,
higher, *Eeee!*

A rat's corpse on a country lane.
Day after day sun and tyres drub it flatter,
greyer; the skeleton powders, and the whole
desiccates, battered colourless;
a pelt of dust that jumps with a breeze.

But just        one second

for the wet joy-shout in Humbaba's throat
to dry to boneless terror

when he sensed Gilgamesh
thrashing through the pages of Creation toward him:
fish, amphibian, dormouse, enraged neanderthal
evolving as he leaps, Eden, the Flood,
bursts into the present, and . . .


We were reined in while they parleyed.
Gilgamesh blagged and promised Humbaba
into surrendering his last Auras –
drawn up around him like magnifying lenses –
for a villa on Euphrates, Swiss bank account,
out with full honours and matchlocks burning.

Suddenly there he was,
beached and gasping, scooped
like a lobster from his shell by the con –
a runty, toss-pot thing like the Wizard of Oz.

The King was for mercy;
but the fool dwarf started slagging Enkidu –
'lick-spittle catamite' I recall (and savour) –
who lost his rag, and stuck him right there.
Who ever loved a magician?

The creep squealed like a peccary sow in rut,
crutched upright for a moment
by a rigid pipe of blood

standing out from his neck –
until it fell away empty,
and he collapsed, gargling a curse.

After all this, our two heroes just stood there,
shifty and nonplussed
like boys caught shop-lifting.

Gilgamesh gave an abrupt, clotted laugh –
like divots startled up by horses' hooves –
as if sudden doubt were racing ahead of it.

Their days were being tallied and weighed;
and they were hot-wired to sacrilege.

We felled the Cedars and scarpered smartish.

Someone would pay.

# Gilgamesh and Ishtar

Peace heavens Gilgamesh on Uruk's walls.
Cinnamon smoke of dusk,
clouds exchanging last colours,
like two women gossiping waist-deep in the sea;

and the faded mauve of palm groves
like tattoos on old skin.
Peace courting time with its perfection.

The incoming, high-velocity blip on the radar screen
flips onto the sky, and cracks the sound barrier.
Before him a Manhattan-high wall of glass air
shatters, and reglazes behind

a woman.
For a moment blue's brakes fail:
everything stammers sapphire
until her eyes cool to human frequencies.

She is ISHTAR,

Goddess of love and lust,
sizzling to mate with Gilgamesh.
She pulses into focus before him:

breasts taut as airships
from hangars nosing,
pearly with the vapour of re-entry friction.

But Gilgamesh knows too well
all her lovers come to a sticky end.

'Radiant Ishtar, to whom, it is said,
very Life comes to confirm its purpose,
let me speak frankly. The marriage you would have

is the annual divine marriage between you
and a consort; that cap-in-hand contract
eking him power for a year,
after which he is fitted for a shroud,
or wakes with an ass's head, braying his terror.

I say it must end.
No more men tossed as hedge-meat to the crows
for one Playboy calendar of nights with you.'

'What?' (Impatient. Her impeccable nails tapping.)

'So Madame, I regret; but no.'

Her mouth darkens, and spits: '*What?*'

Each second he holds out he is hauled up,
another inch,
on the meat-hook of her ire.

She allows a purl of wind off Euphrates
to part her garment . . . so.
Here Beauty comes to draw on beauty for the Earth.

'Gilgamesh, consider . . .'

Man refusing Goddess. A moment
we have so often hoped duplicated,
that smudges of carbon-paper indigo
rub off on our thoughts.

She's containing herself.
Exposed like wine
from which the bottle's been peeled;
only her fury holds the surface tension of her shape:
the slightest breeze . . .

The moment blinks
a pebble into the pool of deadlock between them;
the rings of her anger
expand like the light-wave before an atomic blast;
and race off to the boundaries of Universe
to rake in maximum power.

Then the in-fall of power,
gathering speed across Andromeda,

an optical flaw in the atmosphere above Peru,
a wrinkle of tidal wave on the Indian Ocean . . .

(All, mind, in the time it takes
to put tongue in cheek.)


Between them, at Uruk, stasis.
Phoney time. Motion's rainbow
greys out,

meadows steep in twilight, crickets
ratchet the Pleiades up.

The murmur of lightermen
struggles off the river
like the blurred reflection off waxed tables.
Tick, tick . . .

The tidal bore of the '*What?*''s returning energy
is compressed to a small wave,
a muscle of water rocking their boats;
then changes to a fire-storm in the cane field.

WHAM! the arriving shock-wave
crunches into Gilgamesh
like a wrecker's ball sugaring a windscreen.
She re-forms his clay into tablets,
brands his epic into them,
and pulverises them underfoot.

But he knows, to survive, he must keep it
in his trousers. And he does.

Ishtar staples him with a look
from a place
before life was.

Then she is gone. The icy flame
of her perfume bent in the folds
of hyperspace as it slams behind her.
A bookmark in the great moments
of woman-rage,

as she boils over and steams straight to Anu,
God of the sun, in Heaven.

'I'll have the Bull of Heaven or I'll unzip Hell,
and free the un-dead to suck frost into the living.'

Then, on a pulse, an actor's mood change –
she, pouting: 'Darling Anu,
you know how I'm insulted;
I want, *want* the Bull of Heaven
to revenge my honour.'

She lifts a perfect foot to stamp,
and the tiles of Heaven's floor in rivalry
shift like a Rubik cube to receive it.

What could he do? She is Ishtar,
hips like sultry Tigris,

all drawl and lure;
and a half-smile as inviting
as turned-down sheets.

Reaching over his shoulder
(her left nipple brushing his cheek)
the Lady shears the bolts
fixing the constellation Taurus
to the Zodiac carousel,
and hurls him down to waste Uruk.

# The Great Bull of Heaven

It is night, day's gravity. But this one

is weightless with light,
for the constellation of Taurus
plants himself on Earth,

drowns the plain before Uruk
with brilliance, grazes
the gnat-bloomed, light-stunned
mirror of Euphrates.

There Ishtar, vengeful Ishtar,
blisters her fingers lifting the city
by its outskirts up, like an X-ray,
to a million suns

until she spots the shadow that is Gilgamesh,
and worms into his slumber.

Without waking, the King and Enkidu
seep through sleep's deep rubber baffles,

through the airlock of the city's cedar gate,
out along the slow, insistent
carrier wave of a dream
like their birth-waters,

to do battle with the very stars.


As a reminder, a celebration
of the unutterable beauty of this Earth
we wake to and ignore

the companions leave
the smell of grass bent underfoot,
like a fire in the porches of Antares;
a song of farewell on reed flutes

discarded in the young stars of the Pleiades
whose tall gas-shells wing like sails,
scudding them to creation's rim.


The Bull gores left, tears the continuum's fabric,
opening a time-trap before them.
Together, with out-stretched arms,
they feel the great, winged cobweb of the future
over mouths and eyes,

dragging them in with
scraps of dog barks, pans in the kitchen,

the sound of a wife's footsteps fading
down light years        in the courtyard.


A synchromesh time-shift:
Gilgamesh and Shamhat at the bar
on the tramp steamer *Espiritu Santo*, 1937.
She is dressed like Dietrich in *The Blue Angel* —
sex-crushed satin, décolleté — setting herself up to lose.


Whiff of Abdullahs and quim: designer edge.
From the shadows a steward pushes out
another deep cocktail of hot pearls and lime details,
toward our *übermensch*. See this event as projected


onto a sort of Venetian blind.
If Shamhat tilts the frosted slats with her tongue,
Uruk is beyond, and Ishtar, who has drifted to oblivion.


For who needs the gods when you have poetry
to exalt and redeem man in his fate —
a liturgy without religion?


Gilgamesh, bracing himself against the swell of years
and sea, lifts his glass to honour Shamhat.
'In the frustration of my power-glut,
I ate Uruk's women, then their shadows;
I owned their shadows —
and their sun; nothing that breathed
could sate or gainsay me.
With Enkidu you brought me the freedom of restraint.'

Enkidu sensing their danger –
that they would be sucked from the past and never happen,
loosed an arrow tipped with a black hole
deep into the constellation's hide.

For a local eternity, nothing.
A strand of woman's hair brushing Taurus's face;
in a distant corner of the canvas, a starship, vanes arrayed,
draws solar wind like thistledown. Nothing. Then
the rumble of the sidereal spiral, dragging him towards
the crusher of the event-horizon's lip.


But it was Gilgamesh who finished
the Great Bull;
grabbed his glittering spine and twisted left, right –
jerked it out, and rattled it in his dying face.

Which he did by
opening an eye
and letting the Great Nightmare
Ishtar had cursed them with
dissolve in his morning's
bedside cup of water.

# Enkidu's Dream

The gods filter Enkidu into the circuits
of sleep's glowing encryption tubes:
a ripple-shallow dream deepens to
a CAT-scan, imaging his fate.

Enkidu travels sleep facing backwards
like the retreating sweeper that erases
the burial party's footprints
from the chamber's sanded floor
before sealing the tomb.

And like a swimmer, far out,
under the signs of heaven,
he brushes against the conjunctions of his planets
rising across the wave-wall of his voyage
where he sees himself

floating like a lodestone
in a sea of mercury,
encircled by gods, like many norths,
tugging him to revolve. One

by one they score out his name
for the Humbaba sacrilege.

Lord Anu mouths a word
that twitches him northwards to waking;
and there beside his head,

a print-out of his dream – its message,
Gilgamesh, sitting by his bed, reads and shudders.

'O Enkidu, let us touch while touch still speaks.
Though the word Anu lisped
seemed little more than gossamer,
it is iron, has been stamped on to wet clay
and baked hard as your fate.
It is the word no one escapes.'


If you have seen
those sad films where the gazelle,
certain in his strength to fly beyond
the dawdling hunter,

staggers as the high-velocity round impacts;
stumbles once, twice, and cross-legged
collapses on its haunches, shaking its head
to remove the mistake,

joint by joint sinking
into the sunless howl
rushing up from the grass:

then you can see
the diesel-powered Enkidu in his prime –
at any random time-cut
confident as an express train –

falter like a dawn sensing the cusp
of eclipse bite into it,
when sickness, Death's snare-master, bagged him,
so he staggered, and refused.

And as a man will in fear,
he cursed those who brought him to this:
the Trapper, and Shamhat – even Shamhat,
cruelly, until the lie died in his mouth.

For in his heart he knew the gods
had forged his iron and her silver
folding and welding their layers
a thousand times like a sword;

honed them under a waterfall
to an edge an atom thick:
so was he with Shamhat.

And it was the memory of Shamhat
whose soul is a twist of light and dark
like a cypress unfurling the night stars,
that soothed his dying mind.

'Pray to the gods for me my brother;
read me out with our story;
for the poem reveals a proof
that was always beyond us:

in its imperfect half-echoes
we become the knowledge
that we are the gods,

a moment of creation
exalted in Grace
appealing to itself for more.

Gilgamesh, my celebration, companion,
what is happening? I am a hawk two miles
above you; ten miles to the east I see . . .
look into my eyes, what do you smell?'

'Enkidu, my friend, I smell bread and honey.'

'Yes, my King, I see a child eating bread and honey.
I join you both . . . I am becoming . . .'

# Enkidu's Death

As when words, apprehensive
in their power for careless damage,
are half-spoken, half-recalled;

or snow is mauled, cuffed back
over the wind's shoulder,
and stalls, held up-air,

like a breath hesitating the world
before it falls; or

as a fisherman, braced to gunwale,
feels the staccato Morse of the mackerel strike
telegraph up his arm with such force

that later he will claim he saw in the deep,
the thunderless green, summer chain-lightning
of the shoal:

so Death's arrows hesitated
then struck

on Fate's windward edge,
in slow, ineluctable drifts,
dazing Enkidu's soul

and piercing the blood-roofing armour
of his life.

He sits, struggling to brush off these stiff
antennae of his doom;
then tumbles back into the pillows.

Imagine that drop
as 12,000 feet
of juddering pianola roll,

his panicked fingertips
twisted into the perforations,
composing silent variations
on a theme of terror,
a counter-song to Death's.


Queen Death, Ereshkigal,
of the baying, lidless eyes,
gaffs Enkidu, gasping from life.

Then his spirit-self rustled forward,
drawing around the moment of his end
a curtain of beads and spell-feathers.

# Lament for Enkidu

'My beloved Enkidu,
my self translated to death,
foregone and forever hostage in you.

In the suspended moment
of a crashing aircraft, impact-stillness,
mysterious non-time – through that,
in honey motion, I, Gilgamesh to Enkidu,
turn as a pilot touching the navigator
cross-belted in the tin bucket seat.

My brother, I would re-sow the forests
of flight's principles to save you;
cut out the rotted timber supporting air
and scarf it with my very self;
pit my love against the smoking wires
of gravity, through which the Judges
have reached to seize you.

I will lament for you like the harlot
who anointed you with fragrant oil;

will veil you with your oxygen mask
as one veils a bride.

How long did I slap your corpse-face
to drive a summer into its ice?
Forgive me.
But, O, Enkidu,
how am I to know myself without you?

The complaisant dead inch away,
dislocating the shared vanishing point
of our perspective,
and we struggle to repaint the picture.

Once all mirrors shone with us;
we rose with dawn and stepped into one shape.
Now I can no longer walk round your shape in memory;
forgetfulness takes you
like a quarry-man come to reclaim a statue's stone.

If we are nothing without the maps of memory,
the light is going;
the punctum, sharp essence of another
slipping through the intersection
between the brief latitude of memory
and the longitude of desire.

Yet perhaps it is the dead, not forgetfulness,
who return to collect pictures we hold of them,

as if, like damp photos pressed face to face,
we pull random images from each other
when we separate, carrying them till we die.

How could we know the ribbon of hubris
we hung from
was burning?

The world was always insufficient, my friend;
dithered in the logic of its descriptions,
broke down.

To us it falls to supply the makefaith bridges
– to complete a bird's missing trajectory,
the complex belief of a tomorow – to swerve
its narrative back to sense once more.

And now you are of that unreasoning.
So busy, my brother, so distracted, fashed in sleep
with returning to the grand, dumb becoming
of everything without a voice;

where in the breathless House of Dust
you stand faceless as statues of rain off Gibraltar
as your features smooth – as if I could forget them;

or the blurred, mycelium creep of starlight,
casting your spirit's shade
like the shadowfall of all evaporations, everywhere –
as if I did not know it by heart.

And how do you sleep, love,
now time has looked away?


'This blorting thing I am; this broken hive
swarmed with grief. Yet absurdly,
dawn clatters up its ramshackle geometry
to erect the city again;
a butterfly limbers in its warmth;

above the river a peregrine
explodes a pigeon with its strike –
and none of this is either cruel or benign,
just indifferent – the soughing under our laughter;
in defiance of which we can only
love fiercely and lament.

At the end I was there, all raw alive
and wild to cut a deal with the gods:
mine for yours – but saw no end.
When was the world so casually robbed? What
was the instant you were
and were not?

Missing it haunts me, and leaves you
a body drowned and not recovered.
Uncovered, unburied in water;

jammed somewhere in the heart's reef,
exposed on nightmare's freak low tides,
until I can swim out to join you.

'There were days in Uruk
when I felt I hugged the charts
of all the known love in the universe,
with no room to unfold them.

Now I can't find myself for room.


'Ah, Enkidu, we were the beginning of many things.
Am I not the first to have watched my self die
and lived to tell of it?

We stood with the glow of Eden's river
still warm on our backs;
and before us the river of clay
into which men pressed our story,

in that Mesopotamia of our love.

Will there come a future, with Eden dimmed,
when rivers of new words break into old channels,
washing the dust from our lives
so they exalt in men's hearts again?'

# Underworld

Fill the sky to choking with a reed bed
that rakes across the King's battles.
Count the arrows. Impossible.
Recall, then, their aurora, the spotlight on lurex
of the fletching's metallic shimmer;

their rattle, as a blind of shafts
was pulled down over slaughter's noon.

Nothing. The image means nothing.

Except as it suggests
how the very air at Gilgamesh's side
was woven by his merest gesture to fable.

Or was until he heard of life:
doomed, death-owned – yes,
a twist of hope still – but pointless?
That is the 4 a.m., unravelling word.

Push aside the world-clatter;
stand in the Mariana Trench.
The crush of gravity's paint
flows everywhere.

Half-hear a sound
damped between two thermal layers – then:
the swelling pulse, pulse, pulse of a submarine
towing a glittering hall of bubbles
in its propeller's cavitation,
till void re-absorbs them.

In like wise in the abyss-months after Enkidu's end
his departing spirit cored its phosphorescence
through the rooms of Gilgamesh's sorrow,
then trailed off, dimming, as the shades absorbed him.

Gilgamesh, King of Uruk, Protector of the Flocks,
Lord of the Four Quarters, and so on (and so – back
always to his fear) got drunk, stayed drunk;

travelled rough a smash-and-grab of years
roaring to find a song-line with a pure,
recurving *da capo* that back-flipped before Death.

Or perhaps he went nowhere;
the map moved under him,
and his grief just marked time.

He washed up South as man or God can go,
where the river wades out into blue-causing sea

and blue thrives and unshapes the river's brown
like smoke snatched by the wind.

The madam who ran a road house there,
the veiled Shiduri, Our Lady of Time's Edge,
took him on, and (mostly) dried him out.

We find him there, pushed to the world's prow,
barely more than a beat in the days' narrative.

# The Lady Shiduri

'Light my cigarette, mister?          Thanks.

As I was sayin'.
He just dog-legged in one day,
the air around him popping with anger;
tried to knock the door off its hinges.
Rowing with one oar in the water.
You get used to it in my game.

I sawed some of the crazy off him;
nailed him to a routine.
You do your best:

play nurse doll, hear how it fell apart
with others in other bars
through all the colours of hurt;
uncork a bottle,
evaporate a few years with them.

After I've screwed a man
he can't say jelly-roll but his knees buckle.

Sometimes they never speak again.
But not Kingy.

He never let go – or the deathfear
never let go of him; no room
for my grip on him as well.

When it was worst he was banged up with it
like a rioting prisoner
wash-boarding his slops pail against the bars
*in his head*.     My head.     Enough already.

You getting this, mister?

I told him go see Ur-shanabi, the boat builder,
who knows the waters to the Underworld.
Maybe he could fix 'im up with a trip to Life Everlasting.
Anything to get him outta here.'

# Ur-shanabi

'Lord Gilgamesh,
I will not cross Death's stream with you;
and a boat, well, let me show you.'
(left hand sweeps the bench of shavings)

'Look. From here – to here' (right hand
marks a chalk line) 'keel:
as if you'd dragged your hand across a chart
and lifted a loose run of latitude.

Then, smartly, warp it tight,
an arc clipped to length,
and mortised firmly into stem and stern post
before the tension slacks;
strain it like a bowstring to the ear.

It hums now. That earth-line is a boat's power.
Grab the stress: planks quick from the steamer,
cramped to frame, copper rivets rooved, clenched –
force the tough grain-current to sea-learning.

Sails spread mind on the wind,

crisp sheaves of intelligence
that far out in rain-growing ocean
bend and heel her rasped wet
across blue. Neglect her a point off wind
and she'll knot the sea's shoulders.

But a boat is not what you need.
You have the only means to cross the Waters –
your soul.

Some day when she's close-hauled,
running the long fetch of life,
she'll step ahead of her own breath,

and gather to her way a perfection
greater than the sum of all you could know:

moment that opens onto Grace.
Fix it so, with all you love of the world;
that will ferry you across the Waters
better than anything I could build.'


That afternoon the King punished the bottle
until the spider terrors
danced the edge of a slit-throat
libation trench-cut across his bed,
where crowding shades
lapped with the sound
of surgical tape ripped off skin.

Then, fell and sudden, he recalled
the hunch and moil of battle,
sun's acetylene glare off a full parking lot
of armour;
and those final screams like summer kites
caught in winter trees.

Enkidu at his shoulder, sweet power on them,
they hacked many from life: piston-like, professional killing,
driving them through a glorious red mist.

In the end, sick for immortality,
Ur-shanabi rowed him to the Underworld.
Odd how you have to journey
to death to treat for life.
But then life is not inevitable.

With Ishtar
mouthing his name like raw steak
the gods denied him an undying he.

The consolation was the Herb of Rejuvenation.
When he surfaced in the Upperworld, he got snake-drunk,
and lost it. Everything squandered on one throw.

Yet who, standing in our pell-mell, veteran hearts,
can console us for dying?

After all those tumbledown years,
                              Gilgamesh returned to Uruk.

# Gilgamesh's Death

'From Shiduri's sweltering room I recall:
a sailor, soon ghost,
tarring a rust-boiled anchor on the beach,
a knuckle of sail-prodded horizon,
a fan failing to pull
autumn down from the ceiling.

Fever of distance. The drift of things.
The grandeur in the detail of the drift.

On the river now, time rows beyond itself, taking . . .

what is this thing that carries us
yet evades our fate,
as the spirit of music
evades the guitarist and the guitar?

And of the Underworld, well,
grim it was, but I've seen more terrifying places
in a lover's eyes.

'Now this hour too has almost gone, almost,
like this candle's guttering spear,

a king's last sentinel at the end of the middle watch
when life's tide
debates between ebb and flow;

when couples wake and lie
side by each
to stare at different ceilings,

up into the draining cracks
behind all we do
in the almost gone of lives.


'Last night,
between my name and me there fell
the shadow of Queen Death's owl,
ghostly. It was my call.

So, to wait here,
swallowing this fist of fear in a quayside café
beside these old men
like rows of buttons waiting to be undone,
who rehearse their dignified farewells

against being snatched too quickly to say them;
trusting their shades will speak their goodbye
to those they love:

"Remember me as you saw me last,
gaming quietly with Spiro, my boyhood friend.
It was enough. I was ready when the Lady came."

Lord now lettest thou . . .

I am content at these warm zinc tables,
here among the click and slap-down
of backgammon counters,
like men unbuckling armour;

listening to the soft pencil-hatchings of the evening's gossip
fill in the outline of what we've always known,
but will forget tonight
for the pleasure of hearing again tomorrow;

to sense, just under their tongues,
the ash of many ouzos – and that
unremarked shift

from the determining,
major figurative of youth,
to age's minor anecdotal.

'We are made and broken on a miracle
we look on and cannot see – as though
we had sold out instinct to thought
blinding us to what the world is,
the heart's gate to eternity.

The spirit doesn't exist
because it is greater than existence,
and how it haunts us, the step we cannot take
into that long meaning.

Yet there is an eternity too hasty to last its name,
here where the world preens and marvels in itself,
where poppies salmon up weirs of sunfall,
vines smoke green across walls,
the sea's straw tales burn blue; it is

a spirit flue.

'Lord now lettest thou
thy servant depart in peace,
according to thy word; and befall my soul
that I might follow what is to come:

for mine eyes have seen
the dwindling whistle,
the first steps without a name,
the flesh corposant with love.

In the dusk's quiet, open palm, read
the lifeline of my past intercepting the future.

All I have been crowds, stifles.

I have remembered . . .
almost too much to be.

Such wealth this was

# GLOSSARY

**Akkadian**  Semitic language written in cuneiform by a
people who lived in southern Mesopotamia with the
Sumerians. Their gradual political ascendancy meant the *Epic
of Gilgamesh* was translated into Akkadian, where it was
expanded to form what we know as the standard text.

**Anu**  Ishtar's father, one of the supreme gods; he is
associated with Uruk. At one time probably the paramount
God but was superseded by Enlil.

**Auras**  Their nature is not clear in the text, but they seem
to be supernatural beings or forces, seven in number, that
Humbaba used to defend the Cedar Forest.

**Cassandra**  Trojan captive of the Greek king Agamemnon,
who foretold his death. Like so many of us, she was
endowed with prophetic powers but fated never to be
believed.

**Enkidu**  A wild man fashioned by the gods to check
Gilgamesh's excesses. He lived with the beasts and spoke

their language until Shamhat instructed him in sex and socialised him, whereupon he lost the power to communicate with the animals.

**Enlil**  Supreme deity, god of the winds, law-giving and most aspects of civilisation.

**Ereshkigal**  The dreadful Queen of the Underworld.

**Euphrates**  The westernmost of the two great rivers that bound the area known as Mesopotamia, 'the land between the rivers'.

**Gilgamesh**  King of the city state of Uruk. He first appears in the Sumerian king list *c.* 2800 BC; he is deified about 2600 BC. The first cuneiform text of his epic appears *c.* 2100 BC after a period as an oral poem.

**Humbaba**  An ogreish wizard appointed by Enlil to protect his Sacred Cedars in Lebanon.

**Ishtar**  Goddess of love and lust, daughter of Anu, and the titular deity of Uruk. Her conflict with Gilgamesh probably reflects changes in Sumerian religious practices there.

**Lakish**  A city state in southern Mesopotamia, north of Uruk.

**Lazarus**  A character in the New Testament purportedly resurrected from death by Jesus Christ.

**Lebanon**  Country on the north-eastern Mediterranean littoral, famed through early history for its timber, especially its great mountain cedars.

**Odysseus**  King of Ithaca, Greek hero of the Trojan war. His ten-year journey home is the central subject of Homer's *Odyssey*.

**Penelope**  Odysseus's wife, famed for her enduring loyalty – despite the attention of many suitors while she awaited his return.

**Shamhat**  A priestess of Ishtar. Her role as a sacred hierodule, or courtesan, was a religious one.

**Shiduri**  A wise goddess who ran an ale-house at the rim of the world.

**Sumer**  Roughly the southern third of Mesopotamia, home to the great civilisation of the Sumerians who, at about the same time as the Egyptians, introduced writing, literature, mathematics and a complex and sophisticated culture. Little is known of their origins, and their language, written in cuneiform, has no known cognates.

**Tigris**  The great river, the easternmost of the two that define Mesopotamia.

**Underworld**  The Sumero-Akkadian Netherworld was grim. There was no Elysium. The dead of all classes sat around munching dust.

**Ur**  A powerful city state in the heart of Sumer and the centre of its greatest political period, Ur III.

**Ur-shanabi**  Ferryman to the Sumerian Noah, Uta-napishti; as such he could navigate the Waters of Death.

**Uruk**  City state in southern Mesopotamia on the Euphrates, seat of Gilgamesh's kingdom.

**Uta-napishti**  The Sumerian Noah. After the Flood he was made immortal by the gods. Gilgamesh journeyed to the Underworld to see him hoping to find the secret of everlasting life.